Amazing Science Discoveries

PHYSICS

The story of forces and energy

Dr. Bryson Gore

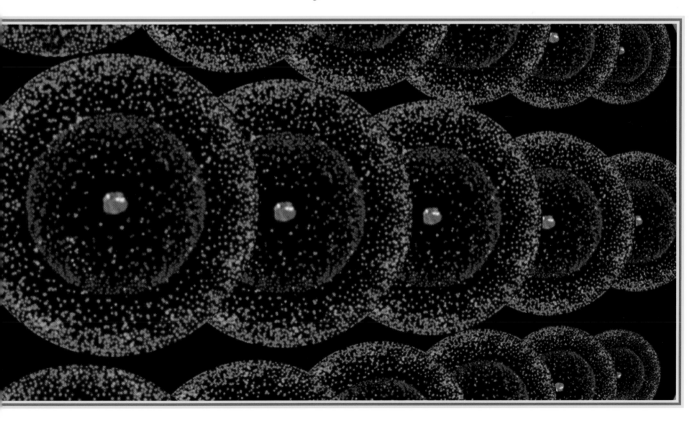

Stargazer Books

Mankato • Minnesota

CONTENTS

© Aladdin Books Ltd 2009

Designed and produced by
Aladdin Books Ltd

First published in 2009
in the United States by Stargazer Books,
distributed by Black Rabbit Books
P.O. Box 3263
Mankato, MN 56002

Printed in the United States

Editors: Katie Harker, Vivian Foster
Design: Flick, Book Design and Graphics
Illustrators: Q2A Creative

Picture research: Brian Hunter Smart

The author, Dr. Bryson Gore, is a freelance lecturer
and science demonstrator, working with the Royal
Institution and other science centers in the UK.

Library of Congress Cataloging-in-Publication Data

Gore, Bryson.
  Physics / Bryson Gore.
      p. cm. -- (Amazing science discoveries)
  Includes index.
  ISBN 978-1-59604-202-5
  1. Physics--Juvenile literature.
  2. Discoveries in science--Juvenile literature. I. Title.
  QC25.G669 2009
  530--dc22
                                        2008016504

Introduction

Humans have puzzled over PHYSICS—the behavior of matter—for hundreds of thousands of years. How do light and sound travel? What is magnetism? We have found out many things about the nature of our world, but many secrets of physics are still waiting to be discovered.

Physics can be seen everywhere. It is the electric light you turn on, or your cell phone, or that big plasma television set in your house.

Physics makes the stars shine at night and the sun shine during the day. In brief, physics is the science of matter, energy, space, and time.

In ancient times, people believed that the behavior of the world was the action of their gods. It wasn't until the 17th century that the great scientist Isaac Newton proposed that all matter was made up of particles, which were later called "atoms."

Newton also developed a series of mathematical laws that started to change the way people understood forces and motion. As each century progressed, scientists discovered more and more about the world around us.

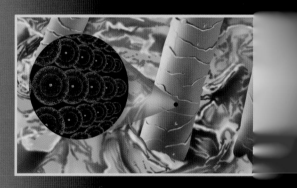

This book takes a look at twelve of the most amazing developments in physical science that have taken place through history. Learn more about the famous physicists and their skills. Use the fact boxes to help you understand more about the ways in which we pieced together the story of forces, energy, and matter. Learn about gravity, the properties of everyday materials, and much much more about the nature of our physical world.

WHEN YOU WALK TO THE WEST THE EARTH SPINS FASTER

Whenever you move around—by walking, running, or turning—you use forces to change the way you are moving. These forces also change the way the earth is moving.

People used to believe that the earth was sitting still because they couldn't feel it move. However, just the same way we can walk around in a moving airplane without noticing it is moving, we can walk on Earth.

West

The science of...

Whenever you move, either speeding up, slowing down, or changing direction, you need a force to create these changes.

Forces change the way you are moving. For example, when you paddle a boat, the force of your paddle pushes the boat forward and the water backward.

We know that the earth spins around once a day, in a counterclockwise direction. Did you know, if you walk to the west you are actually pushing in the same direction as Earth, forcing it to speed up?

Earth's rotation

How do we know?

For thousands of years scientists were confused about the way that objects moved.

In the 17th century, however, the scientist Isaac Newton declared there were three rules:

- An object will sit still or travel in a straight line at a constant speed, unless a force makes it change.
- A change in motion will be greater for small (light) objects and less for heavy ones.
- The force will affect both the object being pushed and the object that is pushing.

For example, a boat on a lake will sit still until somebody, or something, pushes it. Also it is much easier to make an empty boat move than one that has people sitting in it. If you are sitting in another boat, you will find that when you push the boat away, your boat will move backward.

West East

YOU WEIGH LESS WHEN THE MOON IS OVERHEAD

You may have heard people say, "You weigh less in the morning," or "You are shorter in the evening." But how true are these claims? Scientists can prove, however, that we weigh less depending on the position of the moon.

The science of . . .

How much do you weigh?

Did you know that in a spacecraft you would be weightless? On the surface of the moon you weigh about a sixth of what you weigh on Earth, and on the sun you'd weigh nearly 30 times as much!

Your weight depends on the force of gravity. On Earth, the force of gravity keeps you from floating away. That is why when you jump, you come back down to Earth.

When the moon is directly overhead, we are pulled by the gravity of both Earth and the moon, which means we weigh slightly less.

How do we know?

Sir Isaac Newton realized that all objects are attracted to each other. This invisible force is called gravity.

Newton managed to show that all objects used the same gravitational force (or constant) "G," but he didn't know what "G" was!

In 1798, Henry Cavendish worked out the value by measuring the force of gravity between two suspended balls of lead. With this knowledge he could work out the force between two people.

When the moon is overhead, the surface of the sea rises. This is what causes the tides. Two tides move across the oceans every day.

Light and sound are both types of waves.

Sound travels at about 984 feet per second (300 m/s), but light travels at about 186,000 miles (300,000 km) per second.

Light is produced by the interaction of electricity and magnetism, and it does not need anything to travel through.

Sound travels because of the squeezing together and pulling apart of the atoms and molecules in a material through which the sound is traveling.

LIGHT TRAVELS A MILLION TIMES FASTER THAN SOUND

Have you ever wondered why a flash of lightning always happens before a roll of thunder? Actually they both happen at the same time. We see the lightning first, because light travels so much faster than sound.

How do we know?

You can measure the speed of sound using echoes.

Stand about 55–110 yards (50–100 meters) from a flat wall and clap your hands. Make sure each clap is in time with the echo of the previous one. The number of claps you do in 10 seconds, multiplied by twice the distance to the wall and divided by ten, is equivalent to the speed of sound in air.

The speed of light was measured in a similar way by using two lanterns. Today, scientists can measure the distance between the earth and the moon by timing "echoes" of light.

Sir Isaac Newton was the first scientist to realize that white light, from the sun, was actually a mixture of all the colors of the rainbow. He did this by passing light through a prism. Why did he say he saw seven colors? Perhaps it was his lucky number.

The science of . . .

A rainbow is produced when light, usually from the sun, is reflected back from raindrops in the air.

As the light enters and leaves the droplets its direction is changed by an effect called "refraction."

The reason you see the rainbow as an arc is because the droplets of water are round. As the sun's rays hit the droplets, they cause the colors of the light to spread out in an arc.

How do we Know?

Sunlight is made up of thousands of different pure colors all the way from dark red to dark blue.

Humans only have a few names for the colors that are present. To detect color, humans have three types of cells in their eyes. These cells produce a nerve signal when light falls on them, sending a message back to the brain.

Light is a combination of red, green, and blue: the primary colors of light. Varying the amount of red, green, and blue light produces all of the colors in the visible spectrum.

THERE ARE ONLY SIX COLORS IN THE RAINBOW

Most people know the colors of the rainbow by heart—red, orange, yellow, green, blue, indigo, and violet. But did you know that violet doesn't actually appear in a rainbow at all? A rainbow is made up of all the colors of a light spectrum. Violet is just a mixture of red and blue light.

MIRRORS DON'T REVERSE LEFT AND RIGHT

Do you ever wonder if we see ourselves as other people see us? We may see our reflection in a mirror or a store window—but this is just a mirror image. A photograph is a more accurate way of seeing ourselves as we really are.

How do we know?

Look at the picture of the boy on the right. Which hand is he holding up?

The mirror shows him holding up his left hand, but in fact he is holding up his right hand. The mirror has not reversed the image, the confusion is in what we think we are seeing.

A mirror reverses your reflection so that your left and right hands appear interchanged, and yet your head and feet do not. Even if you lie on your side and look at your reflection, your head and feet remain where you'd expect them to be. So why does a mirror appear to reverse left and right, but not top and bottom? The simple answer is it doesn't. It reverses the direction into and out of the surface of the mirror.

We can see our reflection in a mirror because light is reflected back into our eyes.

When light hits a smooth object, like a mirror, it bounces off at the same angle with which it hit the object. This is known as the "law of reflection."

You can make a mirror that reflects the way others see you. Tape two mirrors together and stand them at right angles to one another.

WOWZSAT!

Look into the concave bowl of a spoon and your image will appear upside down. This is because the angle of the spoon reflects light in a different direction.

How do we know?

Atoms are too small to be seen by the naked eye, or even through a microscope that uses light.

Scientists suspected the existence of atoms long before they could actually prove it. The regular shape of crystals gave scientists the clue. A crystal is a solid in which atoms and molecules are packed together in a regularly ordered, repeating pattern.

Dutch scientist Johannes van der Waals discovered that the size of an atom was related to the force of attraction between the atoms.

A HAIR IS WIDER THAN A MILLION ATOMS

Everything in the world around us is made from atoms. Atom are the smallest bits of any substance. They are minute—one million atoms sitting side-by-side in a line would be narrower than a human hair.

Today, there are
around 115 different
elements. An atom is the
smallest piece of pure element.

Atoms are roughly spherical and have a
diameter of about a fifth of a millionth
of a millimeter.

Atoms in metals exist on their own.
Gases and other everyday objects are
made from atoms of different
elements that combine to
form molecules.

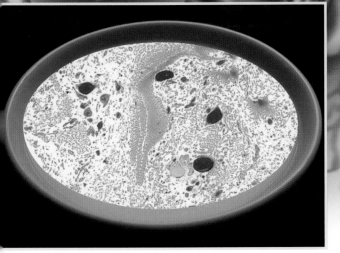

f you take a drop of oil and put it onto the
urface of a bowl of water it will spread out to
orm a thin layer. By doing this it is possible to
vork out the size of an oil molecule.

IRON WILL BECOME MAGNETIC IF IT IS STRUCK BY LIGHTNING

Magnets are substances that can push or pull on other objects. Lightning is a large electric current formed in cloud. It produces heat and a strong magnetic field. For some objects, this is all it takes for magnetism to set to work.

The science of . . .

Iron is one of only three pure metals that can make a permanent magnet.

If lightning strikes a piece of iron, for example a boat or tower, the rapid heating and cooling involved can magnetize it.

Electricity can be used to make a temporary magnet or "electro-magnet." These are useful for lifting large quantities of scrap metal (see the picture on the right).

How do we know?

The atoms of most metals will act like little magnets. However, because the atoms point in different directions, these magnetic forces cancel themselves out.

Certain types of metal and alloys, known as "ferromagnets," can be made to align their atoms and become magnetic. When these atoms are heated, the earth's magnetic field forces the atoms to line up in one direction.

Iron forms a strong magnet when heated to a glowing dull red. If the iron is then cooled very quickly, it can be made into a permanent magnet. Placing a ferromagnet near to a strong magnet can also cause magnetism without the need for heat.

Large iron structures can become magnetic simply by being struck by lightning. When ships are made from iron they can become naturally magnetized in a storm.

During World War II, ships had to be demagnetized to stop them from being targets for bombs and mines.

A CAR USES ABOUT HALF ITS FUEL TO OVERCOME WIND RESISTANCE

Can you imagine a world without cars? With more and more cars on the road and the price of fuel rising all the time, design has become very important. Newer models are built to be more streamlined to make them use less fuel.

The science of . . .

A car traveling along a flat road needs to use fuel for energy to overcome the force of friction so that it keeps moving.

A car has two main sources of friction—the moving parts of the engine, and the resistance of wind that moves over the surface of the car. Making a car aerodynamic reduces the amount of wind resistance. A good example is a Formula One racing car.

Braking, used to slow the car down, also uses more energy than driving at a steady speed.

WOWZSAT

Driving with the car windows open uses more fuel than using the air conditioning. Open windows cause turbulence when moving at speeds of over 40 mph (65 km/h).

How do we Know?

Friction is produced whenever two materials move past each other.

The moving parts of car engines have oil between them to stop the friction.

Car manufacturers also use wind tunnels to simulate the conditions when a car is moving at different speeds. They are always looking at ways in which vehicle design can reduce wind resistance, and help cut down on running costs.

Wind tunnels use a stream of air (with smoke) so that car designers can see where air flow causes resistance.

WHEN GLASS BREAKS, THE CRACKS MOVE AT ¾ MILE (1.5 KM) PER SECOND

We've all broken something by accident, and been shocked by the way in which a glass shatters. Materials like glass are very brittle and break easily because they cannot withstand the force of a sudden impact.

The science of . . .

The speed at which an object breaks varies for different types of materials.

In a brittle material like glass, cracks travel at around 4,920 feet (1,500 m) per second. Because all the energy is concentrated in one area, the cracks travel very quickly.

In contrast, flexible materials spread the force and energy of impact, and small cracks do not spread. In a complex material like green wood, energy is absorbed in producing hundreds of tiny new cracks. A green stick will splinter as more cracks form.

WOWZSAT

Diamonds are cut by making a crack by scratching and then opening the crack with a knife. It takes a millionth of a second for a crack to slice through an average-sized diamond.

How do we Know?

The speed of sound in glass is much faster than the speed of sound in air.

Because the crack is traveling faster than the speed of sound in air, the breaking glass produces what is called a sonic boom. This is what we hear as the "snap" or "crack" as the glass breaks.

The myth that an opera singer can break a glass with the sound of her voice is true, although it would be quite difficult to achieve. Firstly, the glass needs to be made of crystal, because this type of glass absorbs less vibrations.

If you gently tap a glass it produces a high-pitched tone. If the singer can produce the same tone, the vibrating air will start the glass vibrating, too. If the sound is loud enough, the glass will eventually shatter under the strain.

DIAMONDS ARE THE HARDEST OBJECTS IN THE WORLD

The word "diamond" comes from the Greek word *adamas*, which means "invincible." The diamond is the hardest substance known to man. Around 20 percent of the diamonds mined are used for jewelry. The other 80 percent are used in industry.

The science of . . .

One of the most important properties of diamonds is that they are very, very hard.

Diamonds are an unusual form of carbon which usually comes in the form of graphite—the material from which charcoal and lead pencils are made.

If a diamond is so hard, how do you cut it? It is first scratched with another diamond, then cracked with a steel knife. After they are cut a number of times, diamonds are polished to give the jewels their sparkle.

WOWZSAT!

Diamonds were discovered around 2,000 years ago in India. Scientists believe that they are formed some 124 miles (200 km) beneath the earth's surface.

STOP PRESS: In 1985, scientists found a third form of carbon called Fullerene. By compressing Fullerene under intense pressure and at high temperatures, it became so hard that it could actually scratch diamonds.

How do we know?

This is the Friedrich Mohs "scale of hardness," founded in 1822, which is based on natural minerals.

10	Diamond	5	Apatite
9	Corundum	4	Fluorspar
8	Topaz	3	Calcite
7	Quartz	2	Gypsum
6	Feldspar	1	Talc

Today we continue to use Mohs' scale of hardness to compare other materials.

5.5	Glass
5.0	Steel
3.2	Copper
2.5 - 4.0	Pearls
2.2	Your fingernail

The science of . . .

Most materials shrink when cooled, but not water.

The molecules present in ice are held rigidly apart in a crystal structure. The water expands because there is more space between the molecules. When ice melts, the molecules move faster, break apart, and the water contracts as it "falls" into the gaps.

Icebergs float because ice has a lower density than water.

ICE SKATERS SKATE ON WATER

A block of ice can be as rough as concrete, and yet an ice skater can travel many yards with one single push. How can this be? Unlike most other substances, water expands when it turns from liquid into a solid. When the weight of an ice skater puts pressure on the ice, it contracts and melts, creating a slippery surface on which to glide.

How do we know?

Simple experiments have helped reveal the unusual properties of water.

If you take a piece of ice that is just below freezing point (32°F/0°C) and squeeze it, it will melt. If you stand on ice, the pressure of your body will melt the surface and liquid will flow out beneath your feet. If this pressure is removed, the molecules rejoin and the water will refreeze.

The way in which pressure makes ice melt is also what enables you to make snowballs. Snowflakes are jagged and pointed, but when we take a handful of snow and squeeze it, the pressure causes the ice to melt. When we release the pressure, the liquid freezes again, and the flakes stick together. If the snow is too cold (5°F/–15°C), you might not be able to squeeze it hard enough to make the ice melt, and the snowball will simply fall apart again.

How do we know?

Today, we use three temperature scales—Fahrenheit (°F), Celsius (°C), and the Kelvin (K) scale.

The Kelvin scale is the same as the Celsius scale, except that its zero point is at –273°C (instead of the usual 0°C), a figure we call "Absolute Zero."

Although it is impossible to reach "Absolute Zero," scientists have succeeded in getting very close.

The lowest temperature ever produced is one thousandth of one millionth of a degree above Absolute Zero.

NOTHING CAN BE COLDER THAN –459°F (–273°C)

Most of us have an idea of the varying temperatures that occur around the world. If it is very hot it is difficult to stay cool, too cold and we can't get warm. But it is very difficult to imagine anything as cold as –459°F (–273°C)!

The science of . . . .

Temperature is a measure of how much energy something has inside it.

Heat makes atoms move quickly, while cold slows them down.

The coldest weather ever recorded on Earth was –128°F (–89°C) at Vostok, in Antarctica. This is extremely cold when you consider that the carbon dioxide we breathe out freezes at –108°F (–78°C) to make "dry ice!" The cold weather in Vostok was due to the exceptionally high speed of the Antarctic winds.

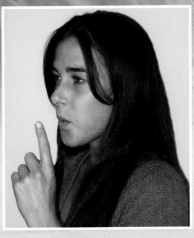

If you lick your finger and then blow on it, your finger gets colder even though your breath is as warm as your finger. This is because water molecules with the most energy evaporate, and leave behind water with less energy which is colder.

Glossary

Absolute Zero—The temperature at which substances possess no thermal energy.

Aerodynamic—Designed to reduce wind resistance.

Atom—The smallest piece of a pure chemical element.

Crystal—The solid form of some substances in which atoms are regularly spaced.

Element—A substance that cannot be separated into simpler substances.

Evaporate—To change a liquid into a vapor by using heat or moving air.

Force—An effect that can change an object's speed, direction, or shape.

Freezing point—The temperature at which a liquid turns into a solid.

Friction—A force that slows down movement and produces heat.

Gravity—The force that pulls all materials together.

Magnetism—The property of some materials to attract or repel a piece of iron.

Mass—The amount of matter in an object.

Microscope—An instrument that makes objects appear larger.

Molecule—A particle made from two or more atoms.

Prism—A triangular piece of glass used to bend rays of light and to split white light into different colors.

Reflection—When a beam of light is bounced off a surface.

Turbulence—The disturbance in a fluid or gas.

Vacuum—An empty space that doesn't contain any matter, air, or gas.

Weight—The force with which something is attracted to the earth, usually converted into kg or pounds.

Biography

Henry Cavendish (1731-1810)
A British physicist who worked out the value of the gravitational constant ("G").

Anders Celsius (1701-1744) A Swedish physicist who devised the Celsius temperature scale.

Daniel Gabriel Fahrenheit (1686-1736)
A German physicist who invented the Fahrenheit temperature scale.

Galilei Galileo (1564-1642)
An Italian physicist and astronomer whose work included the study of motion.

Friedrich Mohs (1773-1839) A German mineralogist who devised the Mohs' scale for hardness.

Sir Isaac Newton (1642-1727) A British physicist who proposed three laws of forces and motion.

William Thompson (Lord Kelvin) (1824-1907)
A Scottish physicist who proposed a temperature scale now called the Kelvin scale.

Johannes Diderik van der Waals (1837-1923)
A Dutch physicist who calculated the size of atoms.

KEY DATES

1624—Galilei Galileo puts forward his theory of the ocean's tides.

1672—Isaac Newton publishes his study on the spectrum of light.

1687—Isaac Newton publishes his laws of motion.

1709—Daniel Fahrenheit invents the alcohol thermometer.

1743—Anders Celsius establishes the Celsius temperature scale.

1848—William Thompson devises the Kelvin temperature scale.

Index

Photocredits:

Abbreviations: l-left, r-right, b-bottom, t-top, c-center, m-middle. Front cover l, back cover r, 12tr, 18-19, 31mr – Corbis. 4br, 8r – Charles M. Duke Jr./NASA. 24mr – Corel. 5tr, 24-25 – Lance Cpl. Samuel Bard Valliere/USMC. 5mrt, 14-15 – Iconotec. 5mrb, 6br, 18bm, 20mr, 22ml, 26t – Photodisc. 5br, 8-9, 18b, 26bl, 28-29, 30br – Digital Stock. 9bl – Flick Smith. 9ml, 29br – PBD. 9b Dr James P. McVey/NOAA Sea Grant Program. 12l – Brand X Pictures. 17bl – Roger Vlitos. 21 – National Research Council, Canada. 22-23 – with thanks to Pilkington Building Products-UK.